BULGARIA

RHODOPE MTS

Xanthe

THRACE

BLACK SEA

W9-CIG-782

10407/72/42

Istanbul

SEA OF
MARMARA

140 6/
30 7

THASOS

MT.
ATHOS

LIMNOS

ANKARA

NORTHERN
SPORADES

LESBOS

TURKEY

AMERICAN BOOK & NEWS AGENCY
A SAMOUHOS
ATHENS
TEL. 818 783

SKIROS

AEGEAN
SEA

CHIOS

is

Marathon

ens

ANDROS

SAMOS

PE
NION

TINOS

DELOS MYKONOS

CYCLADES
ISLANDS

PATMOS

SERIFOS

NAXOS

COS

SIFNOS

MILOS

SANTORIN

DODECANESE ISLANDS

Rhodes

RHODES

CAIRO CARPATHOS

MEDITERRANEAN SEA

Rethymnon

Heraklion

CRETE Knossos

Looking at GREECE

Looking at

FRANCIS NOEL-BAKER

Adam and Charles Black   London
J. B. Lippincott Company   Philadelphia and New York

GREECE

Looking at Other Countries

Looking at HOLLAND   **Looking at JAPAN**
Looking at ITALY   **Looking at SPAIN**
Looking at GREECE   **Looking at FRANCE**
Looking at NORWAY   **Looking at ISRAEL**
Looking at DENMARK   **Looking at SWEDEN**

Further titles in preparation

Acknowledgement is made to the following for their
permission to reproduce photographs:
Alan Wendelken 6, 7b, 10, 18a, 21a and b, 22, 26, 27a,
30a, 36a, 46, 62
Dimitri Papadimos 1, 8b, 9b, 20b, 25b, 33b, 38a
and b, 41a and b, 42, 43a and b, 47a, 50, 51a, 55b,
57b, 58, 59a and b
Feature Pix 3, 23
Gordon Young 11, 14, 31, 55a
J. Allan Cash 20a, 24, 32, 41c
J. Scourovannis 30b
John Stewart 54
Konrad Helbig 33a
National Tourist Office of Greece 8a, 9a, 12a and b, 13, 16, 25a,
28b, 29, 36b, 37, 40, 40a and b, 49a, 52, 53
N. Kontos 7a and c, 15a and b, 18b, 34a and b, 35, 38c, 39, 51b,
63
North Euboean Foundation 5, 17b and c, 49b, 56a and b
P.A.F. International 27b
Picturepoint Ltd. 17a, 19, 28a, 44
V. and N. Tombazi 47b

The photographs on the book jacket are reproduced by
permission of J. Allan Cash
The maps, and the drawing on page 61, are by
Harold Johns

The author is Chairman of the North Euboean Foundation —
see page 15. Visitors to Greece wanting to visit villages
etc. with the Foundation's staff should write to its
offices at Prokopion, Euboea

ISBN 0 7136 0130 2

© 1967 A & C BLACK LTD   4, 5 & 6 SOHO SQUARE   LONDON W1V 6AD
FIRST PUBLISHED 1967, REPRINTED 1971
LIBRARY OF CONGRESS CATALOG CARD NUMBER AC 67–10556
PRINTED IN GREAT BRITAIN BY *JARROLD & SONS LTD   NORWICH*

CONTENTS

The Country

There is a legend that when God finished making the world, he had a pile of stones left over. He threw them into the Mediterranean Sea, and that was Greece!

Serifos

Greece today is certainly rocky, almost everywhere one can see the bare shapes of mountains against the clear horizon, and there are a great many islands. The mainland has a very jagged coastline broken by countless bays and inlets, and it is almost cut in two by the Gulf of Corinth. In fact when the Corinth canal was built the Peloponnese peninsula south of the Gulf became an "island".

There are over 1400 islands and they make up about one-fifth of Greece. The smallest are just rocks. But other islets, water-less and deserted until a few years ago, have now become little holiday kingdoms, lavishly developed by wealthy owners.

The Greek islands have bright beaches, with shady pinewoods running down to the hot sand. The water round them is so clear that when you are swimming you can see shoals of brilliant fish deep down by the shady sea-bed. You may even see a black octopus sprawling at the entrance to his hole.

Dried octopus is considered a delicacy

7

The Royal Tombs
at Mycenae

The largest of all the islands is Crete, rugged and untamed, with rocky peaks which are snow-capped all the year. It is 160 miles long, and from 7 to 35 miles wide. The capital, Chania, has a fine port but the island has few good roads and no railways.

Next in size is Euboea, bleak and stony in the south (though full of archaeological treasures), green and fertile in the north, with some fine forests. Everywhere else the Mediterranean is tideless, but a fierce current sweeps between Euboea and the mainland at Chalcis, changing direction four times every twenty-four hours.

The mainland too is full of variety, with interesting places even in the remotest corners of the country, where *tourismos* is still undeveloped, and where the foreign visitor is a welcome if unusual arrival.

The Peloponnese is Greece's southern peninsula. From its harsh and barren central plain of Arcadia high mountains spread in all directions, and to the northeast other mountains frame the plain of Argos and the ancient city of Mycenae. This was the home of Agamemnon.

Dimitsana
in the
Peloponnese

8

Attica, with the capital Athens and the main port Piraeus, is the most important part of Greece. To the northwest is Epirus, rugged and bleak; east and over the mountains lie the rich and fertile plains of Thessaly. Macedonia, Greece's large northern province, was part of the Turkish empire until 1912.

The Greek mainland is very mountainous. In the northwest and for miles to the south, all is bare mountain. In the northeast the Rhodope range runs out of Bulgaria and Thrace, and down the middle of Greece is the great Pindus range, its upper slopes covered with fir and pine forests, with many peaks over 7000 feet. There are few roads in Pindus, and wandering shepherd families roam the mountain passes with their flocks in search of pasture.

Most of the mountains are very old, the worn humps of limestone peaks. There are many small, fast rivers most of which dry up in summer, or go underground when they reach the valleys. The limestone is very porous, with many impressive caves and underground rivers. In many places near the shore, fresh water gushes from the sea-bed or from cracks in the rock below the surface.

A village in Macedonia

Goats in the Pindus mountains

9

The mountains make travel and transport difficult, but the Greeks are steadily improving their roads and highways. A mainline railway links Athens and Thessaloniki (Salonica) with the rest of Europe, and there are good main roads between the bigger towns. In country districts, however, there are still some small villages without any roads that wheeled vehicles can use, so that the only way of reaching them is by mule or on foot—or, if they are near the sea, by caique (a small Greek sailing boat). Small passenger ships, caiques and motor launches ply between the islands, and there are modern airports at Athens, Thessaloniki, Rhodes, Crete, and in several of the smaller islands and towns. Olympic Airways fly modern jets across the Atlantic, and their domestic flights are growing in popularity with Greek businessmen as well as with foreign tourists.

Greece is full of interesting flowers. The cataclysm which flooded the Mediterranean millions of years ago, and the effects of the Ice Age have produced interesting "evolution pockets", so that many plants are found in one small area only. An amateur Greek botanist recently discovered fifteen species entirely new to science.

One-fifth of Greece is arable land, and many crops are grown, from oats and barley to olives, grapes, citrus fruits and even—in Crete—bananas. The soil is rich in minerals, but it is easily washed away, so that soil erosion is a major problem.

Caiques

Being in the Mediterranean, Greece is a warm country. In Athens the average winter temperature is 47°F (80° in July); the Athenians boast that their city is usually sunny, and it is certainly very rare not to see the sun for a complete day. Throughout Greece, the summer is hot and dry and much of the countryside becomes brown and scorched although heavily forested areas such as northern Euboea remain green right through the summer. In the mountains and forests it is often cool at night.

Scorched land and green forests in Euboea

Because of Greece's shape and position, parts of the country can be extremely cold in winter. Winds sweeping in from the Mediterranean or the Balkans cause sudden changes in the weather. But in Rhodes and on the south coast of Crete it is warm enough to swim almost all the year.

There used to be many trees, and even today one-fifth of Greece is forest. The great enemies are fire and goats. These goats are attractive to look at—though smelly—but they are deadly enemies to trees, shrubs, plants, water, and soil conservation. They belong to peasant families who keep them for their milk, meat and hair—the hair is handwoven into thick coats and rugs, some of which are exported. The goats are kept in herds of up to a thousand.

Libation vase from Heraklion Crete— fifteenth century B C

Most visitors to Greece will of course visit the famous historic sites: the Minoan palaces, Mycenaean tombs, classical temples, Roman cities, Byzantine churches, Frankish castles, medieval monasteries and Turkish mosques.

Greece has a spectacular and varied landscape, a sunny climate, and some good farm land and fine forests. The Greeks are an active, cheerful people who boast that Greek is the only language where "stranger" and "guest" are the same word.

People, Homes and Villages

Greek people are very friendly and eager to help strangers. When you arrive in a remote village you will almost certainly be invited into several homes and offered a meal. This may consist of most of the food in the house, but the traditional Greek villager will quite naturally treat any visitor as an important guest, giving him a good meal and offering to put him up for the night.

Once, an English university professor hiking round Greece was invited into a village home. He was wearing his oldest clothes, and carrying a battered old rucksack, and the Greek peasant family thought he must be even poorer than themselves. They shared their food with him, gave him their best bed, and next morning as he was leaving they offered him some money they had collected from all the houses in the village. Only with great difficulty did the professor persuade them to take it back.

In even the remotest villages there is usually at least one person (often a returned emigrant), who can speak English, and the villagers will quickly find him when an English-speaking visitor arrives.

In large towns and tourist resorts this traditional hospitality is impossible, but in both towns and villages the Greek will ask a visitor all sorts of personal questions: where you come from, your age, the price of your clothes, details of your family, your work, your home. . . . And he will expect you to ask the same kind of questions back. This inquisitiveness is quite genuine—the Greek really is interested in your answers, and he will comment on and discuss them with you.

In a few villages some peasants still live in the old-style two-roomed cottages: the animals (a cow or a couple of oxen, a goat and a donkey or a mule) are kept in one room, and the family live in the other. The floor is made from special clay, mixed and laid by the women of the house.

Some of the family cooking is done indoors on an iron tripod over the fire in the main room. But the large dome-shaped mud oven is made outside. It is heated by burning brushwood inside until the oven is almost red hot. The charcoal is then raked out and the food to be baked (for example, bread) put in. Lamb is the most popular meat, but in some village homes it is still a luxury eaten only on special occasions. Most meals include bread, olives, cheese and vegetables, supplemented by eggs and fresh fruit in season.

Some villages still have no running water or electricity and one of the housewife's (or her daughter's) daily tasks is to visit the village well or spring with a large handmade earthenware pitcher. This is kept in a cool corner of the house for drinking water. Washing is usually done outside in a wooden trough, the water being heated in a cauldron over a log fire.

Even the poorest village home is kept clean and tidy by the housewife, who whitewashes the walls before each important yearly festival. But without running water there is no modern sanitation, and in some remote villages malnutrition and an unbalanced diet cause much illness—many children have bad teeth. Government Health Service doctors and dentists do the best they can, but there are not enough of them, and facilities and transport are often poor.

Epeirus—
traditional
sweetmeats
and metalwork

In one area of 39 villages the North Euboean Foundation has promoted economic and educational development projects and sponsors cottage industries.

Many young men, and some women, from villages all over Greece, leave home for foreign countries where they can earn higher wages and reach a higher standard of living. But often they return home after a few years, having saved enough money to build a house or to start a small business—or, in the case of a girl, to provide a dowry, which in most parts of Greece is still essential if a girl wants to marry.

The Greeks are known throughout the world as good businessmen, quick-witted and shrewd bargainers. But they are generous too, and many villages have hospitals and other public buildings donated by a wealthy local emigrant or businessman.

Life in the large towns is changing rapidly and becoming more and more like that in western Europe and North America. But family life throughout Greece is still very close, and few young men or women leave home until they marry. The husband is still very much master in the family home, and it is still unusual, even in Athens, for a woman or girl to go out to the cinema or to a café by herself, or even with a girl friend.

Throughout Greece marriages are still often arranged by the parents. The young couple do not go out together, and until they are married they meet only in their parents' company. This may seem very old fashioned, but families are at least as happy and stable as elsewhere in the world.

Many villagers
do their own weaving.
Here they are
laying the warp,
preparing it
for the hand-loom

With such a good climate the Greeks spend much of their time outside; most summer cinemas are in the open air, and so are many cafés. The more luxurious blocks of apartments in the main towns are air-conditioned, and older houses have thick stone walls which keep the house cool in summer, especially if the windows and shutters are closed during the day.

In the summer shops and offices have a break of several hours in the afternoon for a meal, followed by a siesta while the sun is at its hottest. Many reopen at five or six o'clock in the evening and stay open until eight o'clock or later. The open air cafés in Athens are still crowded well after midnight, and most people stay up very late at night, refreshed after their afternoon siesta, enjoying the pleasantly cool evening.

A mud oven

Part of
old Athens

A modern
hotel

Athens and
the Piraeus

For several hundred years Athens was the hub of ancient Greek civilization, but then Constantinople took its place and by the end of the Turkish occupation in the nineteenth century Athens was little more than a rambling village, and its port Piraeus a collection of fishermen's huts. In fact Athens had become so insignificant that when Greece gained independence in 1832, the capital and seat of government for the first few years was at Nauplion in the Peloponnese.

Most of modern Athens was built in the mid-nineteenth century, with broad avenues, gardens and squares. Many streets are straight, and cross each other at right angles, making Athens an easy city in which to find one's way. Since the second world war Athens has expanded very quickly, and in the middle of the city big multi-storeyed blocks of apartments have taken the place of dignified family houses, and have even spread out into the suburbs. But in places there have been few changes, and near the Acropolis there are still narrow, crooked streets.

Constitution Square is the hub of Athens, with the Old Royal Palace and the main hotels, and in the roads leading from the square are the University, the National Library and various museums. The middle of the city is dominated by Lycabettus, a steep, pine-wooded hill with a whitewashed church at the top. Round the foot of the hill lies the fashionable quarter of Colonaki where the houses appear to stand on each other's shoulders. In places the roads are so steep that they give way to flights of broad steps.

Today, like other capital cities, Athens is growing fast, and the population of Greater Athens is now just over two million (about one-quarter of the total population of Greece). The city always feels crowded—except at siesta time in summer, and in the very early morning. Everywhere there are little kiosks, many of them open all night, selling anything from peppermints and chocolate to penknives, newspapers and aspirins. Hawkers selling sponges, and others selling nuts, add to the general bustle. Crowds jostle on the pavements (sidewalks) and in narrow streets, the main roads are often jammed with buses and private cars, and parking is nearly as bad a problem as in London or New York.

Buses and trolley cars provide public transport, and there is an electric railway running from the suburb of Kifissia in the north to the port of Piraeus, with a new underground station below the fountains of Omonia Square.

The Old Royal Palace, Constitution Square

Athens has the luxury hotels, smart shops, and night clubs to be found in every large city. But much of the so called "traditional peasant handicraft" in the glossier shops is cheap imitation, and some of the best food and music are in less fashionable places. The open air fish restaurants round the Tourkolimano yacht haven in Piraeus are particularly enjoyable, and nearby are crowded taverns where you can listen to popular *bouzouki* music (the bouzouki is rather like a lute).

The city really comes to life in the evenings, the hundreds of pavement cafés filling at dusk with talkative Athenians, who discuss the international situation and other topical questions until far into the night.

Crowded streets near the market

Athens has more live drama than many other capital cities. In some years the Athens Festival is a major European event, with visiting drama and ballet companies and orchestras from all over the world. Many of them perform in the open air theatre of Herodius Atticus in the shadow of the Acropolis.

Open air cinemas are also very popular, showing both foreign and Greek films. Like some Greek musical composers and poets, many Greek actors and producers are as well known to the public outside Greece as in their own country – sometimes even better known. Greek popular music is becoming increasingly appreciated in other countries.

In ancient Greece, when each city was a self-contained "city state" the Acropolis formed a natural site for fortification, and today the citadel of the Acropolis still dominates Athens. Built during the rule of the statesman Pericles in the fifth century BC, the buildings were still almost perfect until 1687. In that year the invading Venetians set fire to the gunpowder stored there by the Turks.

The buildings have now been partly restored. They include the Propylaea—originally the monumental entrance porch— the Parthenon, the Erechtheum, the little temple of Wingless Victory, and the temple of Poseidon.

The caryatids on the Erechtheum

Ancient Greek artistic and engineering skill was exploited to the full. The base of the Parthenon is very slightly convex, to correct the optical illusion which makes long, straight, horizontal lines under a colonnade appear to sag in the middle. In the same way, the columns themselves are not absolutely vertical: they would appear to push outwards if they were, so they are very slightly inclined inwards. And the outline of each column bulges slightly, because a perfectly straight-edged column would appear narrower in the middle. Finally the four corner columns, standing out against the sky, would look more slender than the others, so their diameter has been fractionally increased. These differences are only a few inches in each case, but exactly enough to make the building perfect.

Now a part of Greater Athens, Piraeus is officially a separate city, one of the major ports of the Mediterranean and an important industrial city with over one hundred factories. The waterfront is always busy, with tourists and merchants, and with piles of fruit and vegetables everywhere.

The port of
Piraeus
with Aegina
in the background

Piraeus has a fine museum, with recently discovered archaeological finds constantly being added.

Athens lies in the plain of Attica, a triangle formed by the coast and two ranges of mountains. A few miles up the east coast of Attica from Athens is the Plain of Marathon where two thousand years ago the Greeks won a great victory over the Persians. News of the Greek victory was brought to Athens by Pheidippides, a famous runner. He ran the twenty-six miles from Marathon to Athens, and this is the origin of the toughest race in modern Olympic Games, the Marathon.

Overlooking the plains of Marathon is Mt. Penteli, the source of the white marble used to build the Parthenon, and still quarried at present.

Tourists visiting the memorial at Marathon

Smaller Towns

Almost every town in Greece has some links with the ancient world. Yet many of those with world-famous names—such as Delphi, Olympia and Argos—are now villages with tourist hotels and the ancient ruins nearby. Delphi lies among the crags of the great mountain Parnassus, and is one of the most impressive classical sites in Greece. To the ancient Greeks this was the hub of the earth, the natural site for their most sacred shrine and oracle. Before almost any major decision statesmen would come to Delphi to consult the oracle. In return they made gifts, and Delphi became immensely rich and powerful.

The oracle's advice was not always very clear—on one occasion she told Alexander the Great to "Go Arrive Not Die", which might have meant "Go. Arrive not. Die", or "Go. Arrive. Not die". But even so wars were begun, and cities built on her advice.

The Treasury of the Athenians, Delphi

Olympia in the northwest Peloponnese was the site of the temple and sacred grove of Olympian Zeus, greatest of all the gods and patron of the Olympic Games. You can still see the ruins of his temple, and of the large stadium and lavish accommodation provided for the Olympic Games. From 776 BC till AD 394 the Olympic Games were held every four years, athletes coming from all over Greece to compete for the coveted title of Olympic victor.

Mystra

Further south in the Peloponnese, on a conical hill near Sparta, is Mystra. It was one of the liveliest cities of the Byzantine empire, yet it has been more or less abandoned since a fire destroyed most of it in 1779.

The White Tower
Thessaloniki

The only really large town apart from Athens and Piraeus is Thessaloniki (Salonica). It was named after a sister of Alexander the Great, and was one of the most important scenes of St. Paul's preaching—he addressed his Epistle to the Thessalonians to its citizens.

Thessaloniki is an important port, with a special free port providing Yugoslavia's only access to the Aegean. The town rises up the slopes of a gentle mountain at the end of the bay, rather like tiers of seats in a concert hall. It overlooks a long quay, at the end of which is a White Tower built by the Venetians in the fifteenth century.

The middle of Thessaloniki was destroyed by fire in 1917, and was rebuilt on a modern plan. But there are still many old Turkish houses in the streets up the hill towards the Byzantine fortress which dominates the city. There is a university, and every September an international trade fair.

Seventh-century mosaic
from the church of
Saint Demetrius—
one of the many
Byzantine churches
in Thessaloniki

Next in size comes Patras, chief city of the Peloponnese and an active and prosperous port. Quantities of wine and currants are exported through its docks. Like Athens, Patras was rebuilt in the nineteenth century and is laid out geometrically. From the top of the medieval castle there is an impressive view of the town and across the Gulf of Corinth.

A daily ferry service links Patras with Brindisi in Italy, via Corfu.

East from Patras is Corinth (from which the word "currant" comes) on the southern shore of the Gulf of Corinth. Controlling land traffic between the mainland and the Peloponnese, and sea traffic along the Gulf to and from the narrow isthmus, Corinth was the richest city of Roman Greece.

It was destroyed by an earthquake in 1858, rebuilt a few miles from the old city, destroyed again in 1928 and again rebuilt.

Corinth canal

Corinth is dominated by the Acrocorinth, the ancient acropolis, surmounted by a great rock 1850 feet high on which stand the ruins of a fortress added to and used in turn by Greeks, Romans, Byzantines, Franks, Venetians (who held it until 1715) and finally Turks. From it there is a magnificent panorama overlooking the Gulfs of Patras and Corinth with Aegina, Salamis, the hills of Attica and Cape Sounion in the distance. The isthmus is now cut by the spectacular Corinth canal, which provides a short sea route from the Aegean to the Adriatic. The canal is almost four miles long, and its sides are 261 feet high at their highest point.

On the east coast of Greece, at the head of the Pagasaean Gulf, is the important northern port of Volos which exports the produce of the fertile plains of Thessaly, and also of its own growing industries, to other parts of Greece and abroad.

In 1955 Volos was partly destroyed by earthquake, but the damaged buildings have been rebuilt and there are now few visible remains of the disaster.

Crete

Crete is the largest of the Greek islands and the most rugged and fierce in appearance, its cliffs rising steeply from the sea, and with high mountain chains along the middle of the island. The Cretans are like their island, proud, energetic and remorseless. Their traditional costume reflects their swagger —it includes a royal blue double-breasted waistcoat with a scarlet-lined cloak, a red fez, and an ivory-hilted dagger in a silver sheath. Few people now wear the full costume, even at festivals. But knee breeches and tall boots are quite common— and much more practical for mountain paths than ordinary trousers.

Crete's main town is Herakleion, a sprawling place, with a fine cathedral and a massive Venetian gate. But the smaller towns of Chania and Rethymnon are as interesting.

Chania is an old town, a jumble of Turkish minarets and Venetian belfries in a landscape of olive trees and mountains. Peasants come in from the nearby villages in carts and buses to sell their goods in the covered market. Chania is in one of Crete's most prosperous areas and from its port olives, olive oil and garden produce are exported. Rethymnon is more peaceful, a town of Turkish houses with latticed shutters. It has a magnificent fort on a hill dominating the town, and a famous mosque with a dome which, according to local tradition, is the second largest in the world (that of St. Sophia, Constantinople, being the largest).

A few miles from Herakleion lies Knossos, the fabulous capital of Europe's first civilization, and of a great empire which began forty-four centuries ago and seems in some ways more refined and "up-to-date" than any since. This was the Minoan civilization, named after King Minos—the builder of the maze where the monster known as the Minotaur was kept.

Sir Arthur Evans, a wealthy Englishman, set to work to excavate and reconstruct Knossos in 1894, and his work, which continued for thirty years, has been complemented by excavations of British, American, Italian, French and Greek archaeologists at buried Minoan palaces and cities all over Crete.

At the sites of these excavations you can see the courts, theatres, processional ways, throne rooms, shrines, store rooms and private apartments of the kings of Crete, down to the smallest detail of domestic water supply, baths, lavatories and drains—and round the palaces, the narrow streets and huddled houses of the cities of four thousand years ago.

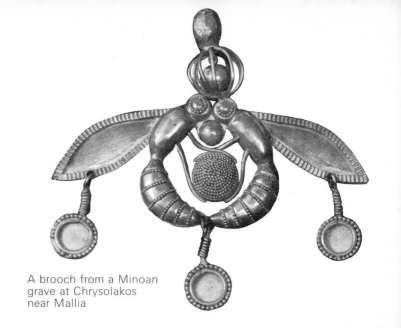

A brooch from a Minoan grave at Chrysolakos near Mallia

Minoan storage vessels from Knossos Palace

Most of the treasures from these excavations are now collected at Herakleion museum—statues, bowls, jars, urns, sarcophagi, frescoes, trinkets, jewels, seals, pottery, bronze, gold and precious stones. From these objects one catches glimpses of daily life at the court of the Minoan monarchs; of smart court ladies; of men and women at work, on hunting expeditions and at processions and celebrations; and of acrobats at the mysterious "bull game". Archaeologists are still arguing about this famous entertainment, the Minoan version of Spanish bullfighting. It seems that performers were young men and women—probably conscripted from nearby lands—who were trained to leap over the bull's back, gripping its horns, and somersaulting up into the air.

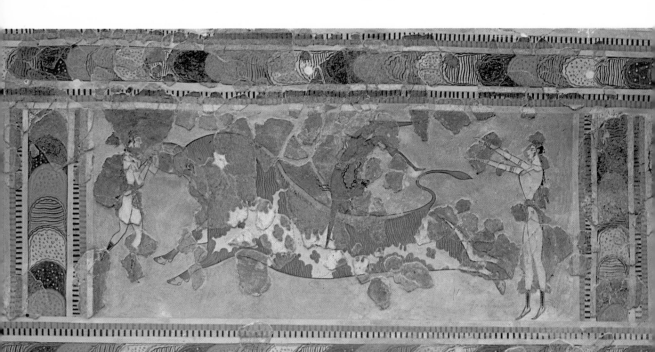

Santorini (Thyra)
a volcanic
island in
the Cyclades group

The
Islands

The Greek islands of the Aegean, many of them volcanic in origin, include three groups: the Northern Sporades, the Cyclades, and the Dodecanese. The Aegean is often stormy and many of its islands bare and rocky, so the inhabitants cannot make much of a living from growing olives and grapes. They rely on the sea, and the sailors have to spend most of their time away from home.

The sponge fishers and divers sail to the north African coasts, where the water is so clear that you can easily see the sponges on the sea-bed. Nowadays the divers use modern underwater equipment, though they used to dive down with a trident in one hand to spear the sponges, and a stone for weight in the other.

Fishing boats at the quayside
on Aegina

Greek sponge fishers have even exported their skill to Florida in the United States, where at Tarpon Springs there is usually a Greek mayor and many Greek traditional customs and religious festivals are still maintained. (In many other North American cities there are Greek communities—usually with their local Greek Orthodox Church.)

The island of Kastellorizon
in the Dodecanese

Usually the villagers' houses are square and flat-roofed, and spotlessly whitewashed, but on some islands they have sloping roofs and red tiles. There are just two rooms, and as the lower one is often used as a store, the whole family lives in the upper room. The staircase is often outside the house.

Many people on the island of Skopelos grow plums. After harvesting, the dark blue plums are left in trays in the hot sun. The drying is completed in a slow oven, after which the plums have become prunes, ready for export.

The Cyclades islands, named after the Greek word for a circle, are southeast of Athens. They form a rough ring round Delos. Most of the Cyclades look barren, but in fact wine, olives, fruit and vegetables are produced in intensively cultivated valleys.

Delos itself is only three miles long and less than one mile wide. It is bare and rocky and has very little water (a problem in many of the Cyclades islands). It is in fact very little use for anything except occasional grazing of sheep, cattle and goats which are brought over by caique from nearby islands. But it is the legendary birthplace and sanctuary of Apollo, and in ancient times people from all over Greece visited Delos to worship at the temple of Apollo. Delos has numerous and varied ruins including temples, statues, mosaics, and the famous Terrace of Lions.

Many of the men of Syra are fishermen. Tinos has a miracle-working shrine of the Virgin Mary where tens of thousands of pilgrims gather each year on her festival, August 15th. Mykonos, with its windmills and white-washed houses, is becoming fashionable with foreign artists and intellectuals, and many of the Aegean islands are popular with tourists.

MIDDLE Sifnos—preparing pots for the kiln
LEFT Mykonos

38

Serifos

The chief island of the next group, the Dodecanese, is Rhodes, 46 miles long and 24 miles wide in places. It is very mountainous but there are fertile valleys where grapes, wine, olives, vegetables and tobacco are produced. The climate is exceptionally mild—several degrees cooler in summer and warmer in winter than Athens—with swimming all the year round.

From 1309 until 1522 (when Suleiman the Magnificent beseiged and captured it) Rhodes was ruled by the crusading Knights of the Order of St. John. The Street of the Knights, with the *Inns* of the various orders, has been carefully restored, together with the Hospital of the Knights (now the archaeological museum), and the Palace of the Grand Master. The massive fortifications, built by the Knights to withstand Turkish attacks, are still very impressive. The minarets and mosques of the small Turkish community in Rhodes were built during the Turkish occupation.

There are many interesting places to visit within easy reach of Rhodes town: the ruined city of Kamiros, with its temples, houses and ancient waterworks; the spectacular acropolis of Lindos, overlooking the little bay where St. Paul landed; and the valley of butterflies where a sudden noise arouses thousands of tiny red and grey butterflies from the dark rocks and shady trees in the cool valley of a mountain stream.

At the northern end of the Dodecanese is Patmos, where St. John was exiled, and where he wrote the *Book of Revelations*.

Rhodes—
Castle of
the Knights
of St John

Lindos
the bay
and the
Acropolis

Off the west coast of Greece are the seven Ionian
islands, the only part of modern Greece never
occupied by the Turks. Corfu, the main island in
the group, was held by Venice from 1386 until
1797 and the houses and narrow streets are
modelled on those of Venice. Unlike many
Greek islands, Corfu has rich vegetation. The
north is mountainous and bare, with small villages below forbidding crags, but towards the
middle the island levels out with lemon, orange
and olive plantations.

Corfu

Education

Almost every village in Greece has its own school for children from six to twelve years old. School hours are adapted to the season of the year, starting as early as half-past-seven in the morning during the summer, with a long break at midday.

Although the weather is often very warm, most of the lessons are inside. But in spring and summer school outings are arranged, either to the seaside (never very far away in Greece) or to a local beauty spot. Occasionally there are visits to a famous church or other places of interest.

The children do not usually play organized games, but physical education and gymnastics are popular, and the end-of-term sports day includes traditional dancing and singing as well as running and jumping. To make the most of the sunny weather, the summer holiday begins in June and does not end until September. But at Christmas and Easter pupils only have a few days off.

Some village schools have as few as twenty, or even ten children, with just one teacher. These tiny schools cannot afford the modern equipment, wall charts and mathematical apparatus usual in British and American schools, and very few of them have even a small library. In spite of these poor conditions, Greek children take their education very seriously.

In the larger villages, and especially in the towns, the schools are bigger, more modern and better equipped, and they have more teachers. Uniforms in the junior schools are of blue cotton—jerkins for boys, pinafores for girls—worn over ordinary clothes, with a school button-badge pinned on to the front.

Many children leave school when they are twelve, particularly in remote areas without a secondary school nearby. The children spend their time for the next few years looking after the family's animals and helping in the fields, especially during the grape and olive harvests. It is very difficult for a Greek boy to get a job until he has completed his military service. This is compulsory, starting at the age of twenty and lasting about two years.

The government plans to increase the school-leaving age to fifteen, and it hopes to do away with most of the very small schools, building modern ones in the larger villages for all the children in the surrounding areas. But first there must be an efficient bus service to take the children to and from school, and a network of good roads (many remote villages can still only be reached on foot—or, in dry weather, by Land Rover).

Secondary education from twelve to eighteen is voluntary and free. But as there are still not enough good secondary schools, many children have to live away from home and few peasant families can afford this expense. If pupils cannot stay with relatives near the school, they have to rent a room, often with two or three friends from the same area. They go home for Saturday and Sunday and return to their lodgings loaded up with food to keep them going throughout the week—or else the parents send food baskets by bus. In summer some children walk to school—it may be a two-hour journey.

Helping
to prepare
the
fishing nets

44

Greek secondary schools still concentrate on teaching their pupils about ancient Greek history and literature. But Greece needs technicians, engineers and mechanics, and technical schools are planned which will teach more practical subjects.

Modern Greek is written with the same alphabet and spelling as ancient Greek and is still basically the same language, although it has become simpler over the centuries. Even the pronunciation is similar.

English is taught as a second language in secondary schools, and no Greek is thought well-educated unless he can speak English.

As is usual on the continent of Europe, the Greeks use the metric system for their weights, measures and coins.

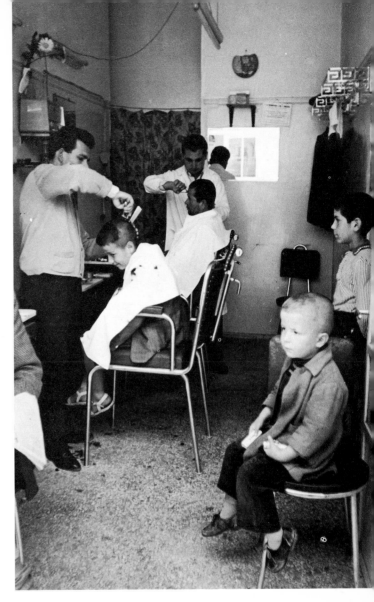

The unit of currency is the drachma: in 1970 £1·00 was worth about 70 drachmas ($1 = 30 drachmas), so a 2-drachma coin was worth nearly 3p, and a 100-drachma note about £1·43.

Most Greek churches have
an *ikonostasis*—a screen
in front of the altar with
religious pictures (icons) on it

Mount Athos, the Meteora
and the Church

East of Thessaloniki, the Chalcidice peninsula juts out into
the Aegean like a trident. On its wild, easternmost prong
towers Mount Athos, 6350 feet high and visible for miles
around. Perched on its cliffs stand the fortified monasteries of
the Holy Mountain. No female, either animal or human, and
no child, is permitted on the mountain. The holy community
was founded in 963 and once had 20,000 monks in twenty
monasteries. Now there are fewer than 3000 and many empty
cells, but the monks have great faith and are sure that they
will get new members.

The monks belong to one of two orders, one very strict—eating the minimum, and attending services eight hours a day—the other much freer. Also on Mount Athos there are many hermits and holy men living in huts and caves. All but one of the monasteries on Mount Athos use the old Byzantine time, with one o'clock at daybreak, and the old Julian calendar which is thirteen days behind ours.

The monasteries of the Meteora can be visited by people of both sexes. A modern road leads to the Meteora, which are at the northwestern tip of the plain of Thessaly. A forest of giant boulders towers up from the hillside, and high up on the most inaccessible rocks are the monasteries and their churches, jumbled buildings with wooden galleries projecting beyond the rock-face. Originally the visitor was hauled up in a net basket on the end of a rope, but today there are steep stairs cut in the rock. From the top there are spectacular views of the Pindus mountains and the land around. Most of the buildings are now ruined and few monks remain.

The monks of Mount Athos and the Meteora belong to the Greek Orthodox Church, as do almost all Greeks. The head of the Church is the Patriarch of Constantinople (Istanbul).

Unlike Roman Catholics, Orthodox priests (except for bishops and monks) are married men, and their churches must not be decorated with statues or images of saints, though holy pictures (icons) are allowed. The local church is still the hub of village life, and the Christian festivals and the many saints days are celebrated enthusiastically. Easter is the most important festival.

Greece now follows the same calendar as western Europe and America, but the date for Easter is differently calculated—it depends on the state of the moon. So the Greek Orthodox Easter is sometimes on the same day as Catholic and Protestant Easter, and sometimes different.

Most churches have a wayside shrine nearby usually on the nearest road or track

Traditions and Festivals

Off the beaten track one loses the iced drinks, modern plumbing, water ski-ing and foreign dance-bands of the expensive tourist resorts. In their place are the hospitality, friendliness and gaiety of the people of the remoter villages.

The small village community still organizes its own entertainment, singing and dancing to words and tunes of long ago. Traditional Greek dances are intricate in step and rhythm. There is usually a leader who improvises in accordance with certain set patterns, and he is supported by a circle of other dancers, a handkerchief between the hands of each.

The best time to see Greek country people merrymaking is after the annual Mass at some small chapel. Once a year, on the festival of the chapel's patron saint, they gather to light their candles at the service conducted by their robed and bearded priest. Then a meal cooked in a huge cauldron under the church council's supervision, is shared out among the congregation. After this, singing and dancing continue until dusk.

Few Greeks today wear traditional costume even on special occasions, though the Vlach shepherds in the northwest still wear rough cloaks of sheepskin or goat's hair, and closely fitting round caps. They speak their own language, a kind of Latin. And in Thrace, where there are many people of Turkish descent, the women still wear scarves wound round the lower half of their faces, even though in Turkey itself women have long since stopped doing this. The men wear baggy trousers, and the fez is still quite common.

Vlach shepherd women with barrels for carrying water or milk

The best known costume is the *foustanella,* worn by the Evzones, mountaineers from Epirus. This is the uniform of the Greek Royal Guard.

Most of Greece's festivals are religious events. May 21st is widely celebrated as the feast of Saints Constantine and Helen. In one village the celebrations culminate with the building of a large fire, and people get so carried away in their frenzy that they run barefoot over the embers.

Royal Guard

Epiphany—
diving for the cross

Epiphany is celebrated everywhere. Villagers throw a cross into the water, and at Piraeus the sea is blessed by the bishop. The ships and port are decorated with bunting, church bells ring, bands play, and there is a carnival to end the day, complete with exotically dressed gypsies and performing monkeys.

But the most solemn festival occurs at Easter. Most cinemas and theatres are closed in Holy Week. Many people fast strictly through Lent, and refuse to eat butter, cheese, fish, oil, milk, eggs or meat. On Good Friday people wear mourning and flags droop at half-mast. The church bell tolls sadly during the day. At night, after holy service, a funeral bier scattered with flowers and rose petals is borne slowly out of the church. Preceded by gilt crosses and escorted by richly robed priests and by the worshippers, the procession moves off among flickering candles and deep-toned chanting.

When Saturday dawns, there is an atmosphere of happy expectancy. The churches are redecorated with myrtle and laurel, and the floors strewn with rosemary. Since the early hours, housewives have been preparing for the feasting that lies ahead and laying in stocks of hard-boiled eggs which they dye red for Easter. By evening the churches are crowded with excited throngs. At midnight the bells peal merrily, fireworks shoot up into the sky, and the priests announce *"Christos anesti!"* (Christ is risen).

52

Easter
celebrations—
Thessaloniki

The rest of Easter Day is spent in feasting and merrymaking. Lambs are roasted on spits, families sit round the table for hours on end, and dancing goes on far into the early hours. Christmas too, of course, is celebrated, though not so much as in other countries, and presents are exchanged at the New Year. Apart from the big religious festivals and Saints' Days, there are also two important national holidays. Greece has undergone much suffering in the course of her long history and has often been ruled by foreign invaders.

Being an intensely patriotic race, the Greeks still remember March 25th 1821 with pride, the day when the Archbishop of Patras raised the national flag and defied the Turks who then dominated their country. This was the beginning of the long battle for independence, in which the English poet Byron also took part. (He died in Greece and is buried at Missolonghi). The day is celebrated with as much passion as Easter. A more recent date, also fixed as a national holiday, is October 28th recalling that in 1940 the Greeks proudly refused to give way to Italy, then an ally of Nazi Germany.

Farming and Industry

Today the Greeks face big tasks in developing and rebuilding their country. As in all Europe, the old way of life is changing fast. Young people move from villages to towns and to foreign countries. Many small villages are being abandoned. They were built remote in the mountains where their inhabitants could escape from dangers which no longer threaten them—pirates, malaria, Turks. Yet even today about half the population of Greece lives from peasant farming—in modern industrial countries the proportion is usually less than ten per cent and sometimes less than five. Already there are large areas of mountains and forest almost uninhabited, and the process is continuing.

Many small peasant farms in the villages are under ten acres—even this amount is sometimes divided into several fields—most peasants have some olive trees, a little vineyard, and a patch for grazing the mule, donkey and oxen, and grow just enough to feed the family.

Threshing corn—more modern methods are gradually being introduced

Farm produce
for sale

Preparing to tread
the grapes
to extract the juice
for winemaking

55

At the American
Farm School
Thessaloniki

The government is beginning to encourage the development of larger, modern, irrigated farms, producing fruit and vegetables, animal fodder and animals, but the peasant farmer cannot afford the expensive modern machinery necessary for efficient farming. As well as government encouragement, farmers receive advice and help from the American Farm School near Thessaloniki. The American school was founded in 1902. It now has 200 students and also runs short courses for 500 adults each year.

Wines, grapes and currants are already important exports. Some of the finest vineyards are in the northern Peloponnese and in Crete. The grapes need hot, dry, sunny weather, and in a good summer the harvest begins in August. On small farms the whole family helps in the harvest, which in some places may take several weeks. The pickers may have to go over each vineyard again and again, picking only the ripe bunches, and leaving the others for a few more days or weeks in the hot sun. There are many varieties of grapes, some for wine-making, some for eating as fresh fruit, and yet others for drying—as sultanas, currants and raisins.

Sorting
peanuts

56

Treading grapes—
the traditional
way of extracting
the juice for
winemaking

Olives flourish in many parts of Greece, but they grow well only in the right place, disliking damp or high positions. Some of the best plantations are near Delphi, and on Euboea. Olive trees are often very old with gnarled and twisted trunks and branches. The olive harvest begins in November. Sheets are spread out at the foot of the tree, and the picker on his ladder runs his fingers lightly along the laden branches. The ripe fruit falls on to the sheets below but the unripe olives do not fall off. As the weeks pass more olives ripen and the process is repeated, continuing through the winter. Not until February is the harvest complete.

There are two main types of olive, one for oil and one for food. Those for eating are usually pickled in barrels of brine. For extracting the oil many villages own two or three olive-presses. The farmer takes his crop along to the press to squeeze out the oil.

Olive picking

57

Oranges, bitter oranges, lemons, and grapefruit are important crops, particularly on the islands of the Aegean. The trees need constant care. They must be fed with chemical fertilizers and kept well watered. From November to March rain usually provides sufficient moisture for the trees, but in the dry months they must be irrigated. In many villages there are special concrete irrigation channels beside the road, fed from a reservoir. The farmer can direct this water on to his lands. On larger, more modern farms "artificial rain" sprinklers are used, the water being pumped from wells by diesel pumps. Lemon trees need watering every four weeks, oranges twice as often.

In some valleys the cultivation of new quick-growing hybrid poplars is a profitable business. These trees have a wide variety of uses, from match making to construction timber. But by and large Greek forests do not make much money. Forest fires, and the goats do not help. But more important, there is little modern industry to use the timber economically in products such as pulp (for paper) and chip board.

The Aleppo pine is tapped for resin, mainly by men who work in the forests in summer, returning to their smallholdings in winter. The resin is refined and used for a variety of industrial purposes including paper, soap and rope making, as a paint-thinner and for plastics and pharmaceutical products, as well as in the traditional Greek wine, *retsina*. Walnuts flourish throughout Greece in valleys where there is enough water.

Tobacco was first introduced into Greece by Spanish Jews expelled from Spain by Ferdinand and Isabella, not long after Columbus discovered the plant in America. But since the first world war the "Turkish" type of tobacco grown in Greece has given way to the now more popular "Virginian" and Rhodesian varieties.

Tobacco—preparing the leaves for curing

59

Shipbuilding yard
at Skaramanga
near Athens

Cotton is an important crop, and large amounts of wheat and other cereals are still grown. But in the future Greek farmers will probably concentrate more on fruit and vegetables for export to cooler countries.

Half of the industry of the whole country is in the Athens-Piraeus area. The government is encouraging industries to start up in other areas, and Thessaloniki is now a rapidly expanding modern industrial town. New industries are also moving to Patras and Chalcis on the island of Euboea, which has very good communications and is not too far from Athens.

In addition to two large new oil refineries at Athens and Thessaloniki and a steelworks at Athens, there are textile works, cement factories, a new tire factory, and a variety of light industries.

Ever since the second world war, Greece has been importing far more than she exports. But she has two other important sources of income which help to pay for her imports; tourists, and the Greek merchant navy—there are now more Greek-owned ships than British.

Classical Greece to the Present Day

The classical age of Greece was at its height from 700 BC to 250 BC, at a time when our early ancestors were still living in caves. Perhaps one reason why the Greeks achieved such a fine civilization was that they realised the importance of educating their children well. Besides learning about art and literature, Greek boys were taught to play the lyre, to sing, and to speak well in public. Arithmetic and geometry were studied, and physical fitness was considered very important.

In addition to this excellent all-round education, Greek boys grew up surrounded by fine architecture and sculpture. The shrines and temples of the Acropolis in Athens must have been a splendid sight.

Europe's politics, philosophy, architecture, mathematics, science, and even her music originated in Greece. There was little that did not interest the Greeks. Most of the terms used today in geometry are Greek in origin, and many of their ideas about trigonometry and optics are unchanged. The Greek scientist Democritus' theory that everything is derived from four elements—earth, water, air, and fire—was accepted until the beginning of modern chemistry in the seventeenth century.

The Acropolis,
Athens
—an imaginary
reconstruction

Plato, Socrates and Aristotle discussed life and death, and rules of conduct and government, while Aeschylus, Sophocles, Euripides and Aristophanes wrote plays for performance in enormous open-air theatres. Seats were cut out of the hillside so that every spectator could see clearly, and the acoustics are so good that even a soft voice on the stage can be heard clearly in the back row. The theatres at Delphi and Epidaurus are still used. Homer's *Iliad* and *Odyssey*, written in the eighth or seventh century BC, are still best-selling books. The *Iliad* tells the story of the last year of the Trojan War, and the *Odyssey* describes the adventures of Odysseus on his way home after the war.

Athens of the fifth century BC still inspires the artists, thinkers and statesmen of the world. The Athens of Pericles was the first really free society (all Athenian citizens were free and equal—although they did have slaves). Before then, and still today in some parts of the world, people were ruled by tyrants, or at least by men or governments who dictated the laws without consulting their subjects. But the Athenians believed that people should be free to make their own decisions, and they successfully ran their city state as a *democracy* (a Greek word meaning "power of the people").

The Greeks were conquered first by the Romans and then after 1453 by the Turks, only becoming an independent country again in 1832. Since then Greece has been at war for 83 of the 140 years.

Epidaurus

62

The Temple
of Poseidon
at Cape Sounion,
on the southern
tip of Attica

With all these problems, the Greeks have taken longer than most European states to improve their country. Greece's first king was deposed, his successor assassinated, and a later king was twice exiled. Throughout modern times Greece has alternated between having a parliamentary government and a dictatorship.

The Greeks are passionately interested in politics, and they tend to believe that every man is equally capable of running the country and solving its international problems—the Greek in his coffee house can argue strongly and persuasively on every political question.

Perhaps this independent spirit makes it more difficult for the Greeks to achieve a stable government. But in any event they have courage and endurance in an emergency, and they are one of the most cheerful, hospitable and entertaining people in the world.

Index